PRAYERS
To Change Your Nation

PRAYERS TO CHANGE YOUR NATION

© 2016 Inspiration Ministries

All Scripture quotations, unless otherwise indicated, are from the New King James Version of the Bible, © 1982 by Thomas Nelson, Inc. Used by permission.

All rights reserved. No part of this publication may be reproduced, stored in a retrieval system, or transmitted in any form by means electronic, mechanical, photocopying, recording, or otherwise, except for the inclusion of brief quotations in a review, without prior permission in writing from the publisher.

ISBN: 9 781936 177318

Published by:
INSPIRATION MINISTRIES
PO Box 7750
Charlotte, NC 28241

+1 803-578-1899

inspiration.org

Printed in the United States of America.

*"If My people who are
called by My name will
humble themselves,
and pray and seek My face,
and turn from their wicked ways,
then I will hear from heaven,
and will forgive their sin
and heal their land."*

– 2 Chronicles 7:14

No matter what nation
you call home, you should weep
for your country as you read
President Abraham Lincoln's
proclamation…

Appointing a Day of National Humiliation, Fasting, and Prayer

March 30, 1863

"Whereas it is the duty of nations as well as of men, to own their dependence upon the overruling power of God, to confess their sins and transgressions, in humble sorrow, yet with assured hope that genuine repentance will lead to mercy and pardon; and to recognize the sublime truth, announced in the Holy Scriptures and proven by all history, that those nations only are blessed whose God is the Lord…

"We have been the recipients of the choicest bounties of Heaven. We have been preserved, these many years, in peace and prosperity. We have grown in numbers, wealth and power, as no other nation has ever grown. But we have forgotten God. We have forgotten the gracious hand which preserved us in peace, and multiplied and enriched and strengthened us; and we have vainly imagined, in the deceitfulness of our hearts, that all these blessings were produced by some superior wisdom and virtue of our own. Intoxicated with unbroken success, we have become too self-sufficient to feel the necessity of redeeming and preserving grace, too proud to pray to the God that made us!

"It behooves us then, to humble ourselves before the offended Power, to confess our national sins, and to pray for clemency and forgiveness…

"All this being done, in sincerity and truth, let us then rest humbly in the hope authorized by the Divine teachings, that the united cry of the Nation will be heard on high, and answered with blessings, no less than the pardon of our national sins, and the restoration of our now divided and suffering Country, to its former happy condition of unity and peace."

CONTENTS

	A Presidential Proclamation 6
1	*Can Prayer Change Your Nation?* 11
2	*Taking Your Nation's Needs to God* 27
3	*Trusting the King of Kings* 41
4	*Laying Hold of God's Promises*. 53
5	*Praying with Authority* 67
6	*God's Formula to Heal Your Land* 79
7	*Is God on Your Nation's Side?* 93
8	*When Light Breaks Through the Darkness*. 111
9	*Prayers for Specific Purposes* 117

A Word from Our Founder 144

We Are Here for YOU! 146

∽

"Therefore I exhort first of all that supplications, prayers, intercessions, and giving of thanks be made for all men, for kings and all who are in authority, that we may lead a quiet and peaceable life in all godliness and reverence."

– 1 Timothy 2:1-2

Can Prayer Change Your Nation?   1

"The one concern of the devil is to keep the saints from praying. He fears nothing from prayerless studies, prayerless work, prayerless religion. He laughs at our toil, he mocks at our wisdom, but he trembles when we pray."
– Samuel Chadwick

The nations of the world are in turmoil today. Economic woes, ethnic conflicts, moral decline, and fears of terrorism present Believers with an urgent need to pray for a spiritual awakening in their nation.

The psalmist describes similar times, when political correctness pits itself against the commandments of God:

*Why do the nations rage,
And the people plot a vain thing?
The kings of the earth set themselves,
And the rulers take counsel together,
Against the LORD and against his anointed*
(Psalm 2:1-2).

But amid this turmoil, we're given an incredible promise about the power of our prayers:

*Ask of Me, and I will give You
The nations for Your inheritance,
And the ends of the earth for Your
possession* (v. 8).

The Lord beckons us to come to Him and pray. He promises that if we *"ask of Him,"* He will give us our nation and extend His Kingdom to *"the ends of the earth."* Rather than cowering in a corner and seeing ourselves as victims in these perilous times, we can go on the offensive through our bold, faith-filled prayers.

PRAYERS GOD WILL ANSWER

The Bible promises that *"the effective, fervent prayer of a righteous man avails much"* (James 5:16). Yet many people are confused about the *kinds* of prayers that God answers.

Some Christians think intercessory prayers have to sound like beautiful flowing poetry in King James English in order for God to respond. Others limit their personal prayers to the level of "Now I Lay Me Down to Sleep," and they reserve serious, real-world prayers for pastors, elders, and other spiritual leaders.

The truth is, God listens and responds to sincere prayers in just about any form or style. He hears prayers that are solemn and reflective, when His people reverently bow before Him. He also responds when we shout or jump up and down with spiritual zeal. Sometimes tears will fall as we wrestle with the enemy over the eternal destiny of the Lost.

The good news is that you don't have to be a highly skilled or theologically trained pastor or leader to pray for your nation to be saved. We're promised that *"the eyes of the Lord are on the righteous, and His ears are open to their prayers"* (1 Peter 3:12). If you have given your life to Christ as your Lord and Savior, you can come boldly—just as you are—to His throne of grace (Hebrews 4:16).

God wants to transform your nation! He wants the people around you to be saved (1 Timothy 2:4, 2 Peter 3:9). And you're promised that when your prayers line up with His will, the Lord will answer your petitions:

Now this is the confidence that we have in Him, that if we ask anything according to His will, He hears us. And if we know that He hears us, whatever we ask, we know that we have the petitions that we have asked of Him (1 John 5:14-15).

You see, there's no need to be timid when praying for your nation! When you pray for a spiritual awakening, you are aligning your prayers with what God already wants to do.

WORLD-SHAKING PRAYER

God's Word says He is willing and able to do far more than we could ever dream or imagine (Ephesians 3:20). That means our prayers are usually much too small. When we pray for the Lord to transform our nation, we typically don't expect much to happen. Yet, as author E.M. Bounds wrote many years ago, "The church on its knees would bring Heaven upon the earth."

Prayer not only can transform your personal life and the lives of your loved ones, but it can also transform your church, your community, your nation, and even other countries.

Early in the last century, a world-shaking revival broke out in a dilapidated building at 312 Azusa Street in Los Angeles. Only a few hundred people could fit into the "Azusa Street Mission," but repercussions were felt around the world as the Holy Spirit touched lives and brought dramatic healings for nearly three years. What started as a prayer meeting attended by a handful of spiritually thirsty believers has grown into the fastest-growing segment of Christianity today—with an estimated 600 million adherents.

What brought about this remarkable move of the Holy Spirit? The human leadership of the revival was clearly unimpressive by worldly standards. One of the leaders mightily used by God was William J. Seymour, an uneducated preacher who grew up in poverty as the son of former slaves. Before entering the ministry, Seymour was a railroad porter and a waiter at several restaurants. Smallpox had left him blind in one eye.

Eye-witness accounts of the Azusa Street Revival say little about Seymour's preaching or leadership skills—for those attributes weren't the secret to his effectiveness. Here's how one Los Angeles newspaper described Seymour's role:

> Their preacher [Seymour] stays on his knees much of the time with his head hidden between the wooden milk crates. He doesn't talk very much, but at times he can be heard shouting "Repent"—and he's supposed to be running the thing...

The breakthrough at Azusa Street clearly wasn't the result of great preaching, marketing techniques, financial backing, or organizational skills. Instead, the secret of the Azusa Street Revival's *world-shaking power* was simply this: *world-shaking prayer*. It was sparked not by brilliant *theology* but by passionate and persistent *knee-ology*. The very same power is available today—if we're willing to pay the price.

PRAYING WITH PASSION

William J. Seymour and the fledgling band of Christians at Azusa Street didn't pray lukewarm, passionless, or unbelieving prayers. Their prayers arose from an intense burden for new intimacy with God…for a breakthrough of power from on high…and for SOULS. Instead of the polite but powerless prayers we so often hear today, these believers were *desperate* in their intercession—often groaning for hours before the throne of God.

We say we want God to move powerfully in our lives, but where are the prayer warriors today who will cry out as Isaiah did: *"Oh, that You would rend the heavens and come down!"* (Isaiah 64:1)? To shake the earth, we need prayers that will *"rend the heavens."* We need *breakthrough* prayers!

God's heart breaks over the condition of the Lost, and He wants *our* hearts to break as well. Look at the Apostle Paul's anguish for the Jewish people who had not yet met Jesus as their Messiah:

> *I have great sorrow and unceasing grief in my heart. For I could wish that I myself*

were accursed, separated from Christ for the sake of my brethren, my kinsmen according to the flesh, who are Israelites… (Romans 9:1-4).

Do *we* have this kind of heartache as we consider the lost Souls sitting in darkness in the nations of the world? Are our passionate prayers of intercession ascending to God? Do we regularly plant sacrificial financial seeds to send the light of the Gospel around the world?

Despite a seeming lack of human credentials, charisma, or resources, God heard the prayers of the Believers who met at the small building on Azusa Street. The resulting move of the Holy Spirit sent a tidal wave of transformation around the world—still impacting lives today.

In the same way, we have an incredible opportunity to shatter the darkness in the world today when we apply God's scriptural principles to our intercession for the nation in which we live. Your prayers are important to God. He longs to receive *your* intercession for *your* nation. And this booklet was written to give you the tools you need to make your prayers more effective.

SHAKING THE NATIONS

What does world-shaking prayer look like? In addition to the outpouring of the Holy Spirit at Pentecost (Acts 2), the early Christians experienced several other "power encounters" in response to their prayers:

> *When they had **prayed**, the place where they had gathered together was **shaken**, and they were all filled with the Holy Spirit and began to speak the word of God with **boldness*** (Acts 4:31).

While we might be awestruck at the *physical* shaking that occurred after these believers prayed, that was only a by-product of something much more important: They experienced a fresh encounter with God and new boldness to proclaim the Gospel. The church today needs this same kind of supernatural encounter with the Holy Spirit, but it will only happen as we give ourselves to passionate intercession, as the early believers did.

Sometimes our world-shaking prayers will arise from very difficult situations, as Paul and Silas experienced in the Philippian jail:

*About midnight Paul and Silas were **praying** and **singing hymns of praise** to God…and suddenly there came a great **earthquake**, so that **the foundations of the prison house were shaken**; and immediately all the **doors** were opened and everyone's **chains** were unfastened* (Acts 16:25-27).

Paul and Silas weren't *trying* to cause an earthquake, but simply were focusing their hearts on prayer and worship. Yet the result was a mighty shaking—not only in the earthly realm but also in the unseen realm of the Spirit.

It's significant that *"doors were opened"* and *"chains were unfastened"* as a result of their prayers and praises. Do *you* need doors to open in your life or the lives of your loved ones? Are you, your children, or your grandchildren shackled by the enemy in some area of health, finances, relationships, or peace of mind? Then it's time for world-shaking prayer and worship!

OUR NEED FOR REVIVAL TODAY

The revival on Azusa Street was just one of many spiritual awakenings God has brought throughout the centuries. Each of these was unique in many ways, yet there also were similarities. Nineteenth-century American revivalist Charles Finney summarized the essence of revival as nothing more than "a new beginning of obedience to God." And New England preacher Jonathan Edwards, a key leader in the First Great Awakening in 1733 to 1735, said, "The heart of true religion is holy affection…Our people do not so much need to have their heads stored, as to have their hearts touched."

Revival won't come unless there is more *yearning* and less *yawning*. Instead of being content on the spiritual plateau we've reached, we must hunger and thirst for more of God's presence in our lives (Psalm 42:1-3, Matthew 5:6, Philippians 3:12-15). Our impact on the world will skyrocket when we return to our first love and cast aside apathy and lukewarmness (Revelation 2:1-5, Revelation 3:14-22).

British Bible teacher Arthur Wallis wrote in

his book, *In the Day of Thy Power*, "The spiritual labors of 50 years can be surpassed in so many days when the Spirit is poured out." However, Wallis points out that this observation raises inescapable questions:

> If God can achieve such mighty things in times of revival, and if the spiritual labors of 50 years can be surpassed in so many days when the Spirit is poured out, why is the church today so satisfied with the results of normal evangelism? Why are we not more concerned that there should be another great revival? Why do we not pray for it day and night?

The great revivals of the past shook nations. Bars shut down. Prostitution became unprofitable. The jails were nearly empty because crime practically stopped. The very foundations of the church and the surrounding society were shaken.

In addition to experiencing revival at several times in his own life, Wallis described a number of amazing spiritual awakenings in previous centuries:

- Under the leadership of Count von Zinzendorf and others, the Moravians launched a prayer movement that included uninterrupted intercession, 24 hours a day, for 100 years. Missionaries were sent around the world to spread the Gospel and establish Christian communities.

- Revivals around Rochester, New York, in the early 1830s resulted in between 50,000 to 100,000 conversions in a little over a year. From 1830 to 1835, approximately 200,000 people were saved in that area. Many of these were the result of Charles Finney's ministry, 80% of whose converts remained true to the Lord and a part of a church.

- In 1857, Jeremiah Lanphier started a prayer meeting in New York City, and only six people attended the first week. But within six months, 10,000 businessmen were gathering for prayer daily throughout the city.

Despite its humble beginnings, this prayer movement spread across the world. For two years, an average of 10,000 people each week were giving their lives to Christ for the first time.

- In the Welsh revival, over 70,000 converts were reported in just a few months, during 1904 and 1905. The awakening swept through the rest of Britain, Scandinavia, parts of Europe, North America, India and the Orient, Africa, and Latin America.

When you're praying for a spiritual awakening, pray BIG prayers! The same God who transformed communities, cities, and nations during past revivals can do great things again when His people pray.

TIPS FOR STARTING A REVIVAL

A young man once asked an old preacher how he could start a revival. The old man of God replied, "Young man, all it takes is a piece of chalk."

"I don't understand," the young man replied

with a puzzled look on his face. "What does chalk have to do with triggering a spiritual awakening?"

"Just get a piece of chalk and draw a circle on the floor around your feet," the old preacher said with a chuckle. "Then cry out to God with all your heart: 'Lord, revive the person in this circle!' When the Lord answers your prayer, revival has begun!"

It's amazing what a piece of chalk can do when coupled with persistent, honest prayer for a fresh move of God. Are you willing to test the old preacher's advice?

London pastor Charles Spurgeon gave a similar recommendation to a young preacher who asked him to attract larger crowds to hear his messages: "Young man, just set yourself on fire, and people will gather around to watch you burn!"

Taking Your Nation's Needs to God

2

"Our praying...needs to be pressed and pursued with an energy that never tires, a persistency which will not be denied, and a courage which never fails."

– E.M. Bounds

If you were introduced to the president of your country or to a famous celebrity, you probably would speak with more reverence than you would to your children while sitting at home around the dinner table. By God's very nature, you should want to revere Him, honor Him, and offer Him your best, even when that means your best words in prayer.

God is pure, holy, and mighty. He wants you

to approach Him boldly, as Jesus's death on the cross gave you the right to do (Hebrews 10:19-23). But at the same time, He wants you to experience His majesty and recognize that He's the Creator of everything in Heaven and on earth. That means coming before His presence with reverence and humility.

When you pray, God promises He is right there beside you. It's remarkable that the Creator of the universe even wants to have fellowship with us, yet He says He delights in our praises and longs for us to come to Him in prayer. He wants us to lay our burdens down before His throne and cast our cares upon Him—because He cares passionately about us (1 Peter 5:7).

God also cares about your nation. Why? Because He loves people. He knows that good leaders in a nation will enable His people to *"lead a quiet and peaceable life"* (1 Timothy 2:2). When a nation submits to God's precepts, the result is blessings for its people: *"Blessed is the nation whose God is the LORD"* (Psalm 33:12).

This means there are tangible benefits when your prayers help to change your nation. When more of God's Kingdom is manifested (Matthew 6:10), the result will be a better life for you, your children, your grandchildren, and even the coming generations.

Don't neglect your own personal time of prayer with the Lord each day! Your daily times of prayer and worship can play an important role in keeping you from slipping into fear, anxiety, depression, confusion, or turmoil. As you cast your personal burdens on the Lord and leave them at the foot of the cross of Christ every day, you'll be in a much better position to pray for your nation.

REAPING IN DUE SEASON

When you pray for your nation, it can be easy to become discouraged if you don't see results right away. Yet Galatians 6:9 reminds us, *"Let us not grow weary while doing good, for in due season we shall reap if we do not lose heart."* Sometimes the harvest we're praying for will require great patience, and at times it won't even come in our lifetime.

W.C. Burns was a Scottish preacher and intercessor who saw entire cities shake with revival across Scotland in the early 1800s. The revival touched lives in schools, businesses, and on the streets. People seldom talked about sports during their leisure time, because they were too busy speaking of the marvelous works of God in transforming their community.

At the height of his work in Scotland, Burns felt called to China. But although he prayed and interceded for China diligently for several years, nothing happened like the miraculous transformation he had seen in Scottish cities. But he never gave up. He was never shaken from his call to intercede for the Chinese people.

W.C. Burns is not typically one of the missionaries we remember today, but his hidden work plowed the fallow ground of China so that another missionary, Jonathan Goforth, could go in and reap a harvest of souls for the Kingdom of God after Burns died.

Burns' last words were "Thine is the kingdom, the power, and the glory forever and ever."

He had been faithful, yet he never witnessed the impact his intercession would one day have on China.

Interceding for your nation is a high calling. Although taking on this prayer burden may seem overwhelming at times, you can take small steps every day in your personal prayer time. Seldom does the answer come right away, but don't let that discourage you.

PRAYING FOR SPIRITUAL RAIN

In some ways, interceding for a spiritual awakening is similar to the prophet Elijah's experience when praying for rain after Israel's three years of drought:

Elijah said to Ahab, "Go up, eat and drink; for there is the sound of abundance of rain." So Ahab went up to eat and drink. And Elijah went up to the top of Carmel; then he bowed down on the ground, and put his face between his knees, and said to his servant, "Go up now, look toward the sea."

So he went up and looked, and said,

"There is nothing." And seven times he said, "Go again."

Then it came to pass the seventh time, that he said, "There is a cloud, as small as a man's hand, rising out of the sea!" So he said, "Go up, say to Ahab, 'Prepare your chariot, and go down before the rain stops you.'"

Now it happened in the meantime that the sky became black with clouds and wind, and there was a heavy rain (1 Kings 18:41-45).

At the beginning of this passage, Elijah proclaimed to King Ahab, *"There is the sound of abundance of rain."* Actually, this was just a faith declaration, because there were absolutely no signs of rain on the horizon. In the same way, with our eyes of faith we need to see revival coming. Perhaps no one else will believe us at first, but we need to declare that God will be faithful to honor our prayers.

Our words are powerful, able to create either life or death (Proverbs 18:21). Like Elijah, we should declare that spiritual rain showers are on the way, even when there is not yet any evidence.

Next, Elijah told his servant to go look for signs of storm clouds. Six times, the servant came back and told him, "There is nothing." But Elijah refused to give up. He kept sending his servant back to look again.

Finally, the servant saw something the seventh time: *"There is a cloud, as small as a man's hand, rising out of the sea!"*

God had heard Elijah's prayers, just as he knew God would. *"The sky became black with clouds and wind, and there was a heavy rain."*

How long have you been praying for a spiritual awakening in your nation? Perhaps you still don't even see a cloud in the sky. Or maybe there's just a tiny cloud on the horizon, not giving you much cause for optimism.

Nevertheless, it's time to declare God's Word and believe His promises. If you're praying, meeting God's conditions, and speaking words of faith, a spiritual downpour is on the way.

DEATH TO SELF

Although it may sound exciting to hear about the possibility of revival in your country, remember that there's a price to pay. The call to lay down your life in powerful intercession is sure to require some death to self.

Jesus explained why dying to ourselves is such an important ingredient in gaining a fruitful harvest:

Truly, truly, I say to you, unless a grain of wheat falls into the earth and dies, it remains alone; but if it dies, it bears much fruit (John 12:24 NASB).

Jesus laid down His life, dying for our sins so we could have a relationship with the Father. He calls us to lay down *our* lives as well. The Apostle Paul spoke of dying to ourselves when he wrote, *"I die daily"* (1 Corinthians 15:31) and *"I have been crucified with Christ; and it is no longer I who live, but Christ lives in me"* (Galatians 2:20).

As we make nation-changing intercession a priority, there will be times when we must die to our own interests and pursuits. But the result will be *"much fruit"* as people come to Christ and our cities are transformed.

Before your breakthroughs come, there often will be long periods when you wonder if anything is happening. A seed that you've planted in the ground won't spring up overnight. You can sow watermelon seeds one day and expect the harvest to be ready the next day. Don't give up during the season of *waiting*! God is working behind the scenes, even when you can't see what He is doing.

REFUSING TO GIVE UP

Hebrews 6:12 says we inherit God's promises through *"faith and **patience**"*—not faith alone! That's why perseverance is one of the most important ingredients for answered prayer.

In Luke 18:1-8, Jesus says we *"always ought to pray and not lose heart."* He goes on to tell the story of a woman who wouldn't stop pounding on the judge's door until she got a response, and that's exactly the posture we must take as we intercede for our city and nation. We need to pound on Heaven's door until we see God's answer.

Jesus promises us:

Ask, and it will be given to you; seek, and you will find; knock, and it will be opened to you. For everyone who asks receives, and he who seeks, finds, and to him who knocks, it will be opened (Luke 11:9-10).

The literal Greek translation of this passage says, *"Ask and **keep on** asking…seek and **keep on** seeking…knock and **keep on** knocking."* We must pray and keep on praying. We must never give up!

Scripture tells us that Satan is like a restless, starving, roaring lion, pacing about and searching for victims to devour (1 Peter 5:8-9). He never stops prowling, so we must never stop praying. Our prayers are our greatest weapon as we wage war on behalf of God's Kingdom.

Even when things seem to get worse before they get better, never forget that God and His mercies are new every morning (Lamentations 3:21-23). He loves you, your loved ones, your city, and your nation more than you can comprehend. You can trust Him 100% with your future…and theirs.

So ask and keep on asking…seeking…knocking…praying. Keep believing, keep trusting, and you *WILL* see God's goodness and faithfulness in answering your prayers:

Wait on the LORD and be of good courage, and He shall strengthen your heart; wait, I say, on the LORD (Psalm 27:14).

UNITED PRAYER

King David provides us with another important key to nation-changing prayers:

How good and pleasant it is when God's people live together in unity!

It is like precious oil poured on the head, running down on the beard,

running down on Aaron's beard, down on the collar of his robe.

It is as if the dew of Hermon were falling on Mount Zion.

For there the LORD bestows his blessing, even life forevermore (Psalm 133:1-3).

When there is unity among God's people, our prayers have great impact and *"the Lord bestows his blessing."* However, when there is strife and disunity, our prayers are undercut and our testimony to the watching world is weakened (John 17:21-22).

Yes, your personal prayers are powerful—but they're much *more* powerful when joined in harmony with other Believers. Deuteronomy 32:30 makes the amazing statement that one person can *"chase a thousand"* of the enemy army, but two people can *"put ten thousand to flight."* There's synergy when we pray together, greatly multiplying our effectiveness.

Jesus described this same principle in Matthew 18:18-20:

> *Whatever you bind on earth will be bound in heaven, and whatever you loose on earth will be loosed in heaven. Again I say to you that if two of you agree on earth concerning anything that they ask, it will be done for them by My Father in heaven. For where two or three are gathered together in My name, I am there in the midst of them.*

It's no accident that the Holy Spirit was poured out on the Day of Pentecost when the Believers gathered together in one accord to pray and worship the Lord (Acts 2:1-4). Just a few days earlier, Jesus' disciples had felt discouraged and defeated, but everything changed when they were empowered by the Spirit:

Suddenly there came a sound from heaven, as of a rushing mighty wind, and it filled the whole house where they were sitting. Then there appeared to them divided tongues, as of fire, and one sat upon each of them. And they were all filled with the Holy Spirit and began to speak with other tongues, as the Spirit gave them utterance.

In nearly every nation, the church today is in desperate need of fresh fire to empower us to fulfill the Great Commission. The only way that will happen is if Believers join their prayers together in united, purposeful intercession.

Trusting the King of Kings 3

"Intercessory prayer is exceedingly prevalent. What wonders it has wrought! The Word of God teems with its marvelous deeds. Believer, you have a mighty engine in your hand—use it well, use it constantly, use it with faith, and you shall surely be a benefactor to your brethren."
– Charles Spurgeon

A critical step in your role as an intercessor is recognizing God's sovereignty and then relinquishing your nation into His hands. The changes that need to happen will not be the result of human effort or ingenuity, but rather will come by a mighty move of the Spirit of God.

As *"the King of kings and Lord of lords"*

(1 Timothy 6:15), God has no limitations. He *"works all things according to the counsel of His will"* (Ephesians 1:11), and *"in Him all things hold together"* (Colossians 1:17 NASB).

Nothing is impossible for the Lord (Jeremiah 32:17). Isaiah 46:11 says that if He *speaks* something, He will *do* it. And when He *purposes* something, it is certain to come to pass.

The psalmist reminds us that *"our God is in heaven; He does whatever He pleases"* (Psalm 115:3). In other words, God is God—and we are *not*.

God is the Potter, and we are merely the clay (Isaiah 45:9). Yet He is intent on working all things together for our good (Romans 8:28).

Even when it looks like the world is totally out of control, our God *"rules over the nations"* (Psalm 22:28), and He establishes the governing authorities on earth (Romans 13:1). And although many earthly leaders openly reject God's authority, He can still change their direction at any time He chooses: *"The king's heart is in the hand of the Lord, like the rivers of water; He turns it wherever He wishes"* (Proverbs 21:1).

When you are interceding for your city and your nation, it's important for you to be grounded in these truths about your all-powerful, all-knowing, all-wise God. One word from Him can transform your personal circumstances or the entire trajectory of your nation!

GOD'S LOVING PLAN

The Lord loves your loved ones, neighbors, and friends even more than you do. He wants to save them…heal them…bless them. In fact, one of the most popular verses in the Bible speaks of God's plans to bless your city and your nation:

> *"'I know the plans I have for you,' declares the LORD, 'plans to prosper you and not to harm you, plans to give you hope and a future'"* (Jeremiah 29:11).

Yes, Jeremiah 29:11 is a great promise to claim for yourself and your loved ones. But the context is actually much different than that. The verse comes amid a chapter where God was challenging His people to seek blessings and favor on the nation where they were exiled.

The backdrop of Jeremiah 29 is that Jerusalem had been invaded by a fierce enemy army from Babylon. Many Israelites had been taken captive and forcibly removed to the capital city of the invading nation. The Israelites were proud and independent-minded people, of course, and weren't inclined to accept this fate without a struggle.

Yet God has plans for His people, even at such times as this. While many of the leaders advocated some form of rebellion or escape, Jeremiah was the lone prophetic voice who offered this unthinkable advice:

Build houses and settle down; plant gardens and eat what they produce. Marry and have sons and daughters; find wives for your sons and give your daughters in marriage, so that they too may have sons and daughters. Increase in number there; do not decrease.

Also, **seek the peace and prosperity of the city** *to which I have carried you into exile.* **Pray to the LORD for it, because if it prospers, you too will prosper** (Jeremiah 29:5-7).

At such advice, you might have protested, "Are you crazy! Why in the world would we want to ask God to grant peace and blessing to our captors?"

You see, no matter what nation you may be living in, this world is not your ultimate home. You are living in a foreign land, not the Kingdom of God. But as a citizen of Heaven, you are called to be a Heavenly ambassador to a world that desperately needs to be reconciled to God (Philippians 3:20, 2 Corinthians 5:20). And, as Jeremiah told the Israelites who were living in Babylon, you need to pray for your city and nation. Why? *"Because if it prospers, you too will prosper."*

SEEKING FIRST THE KINGDOM

In a section of the Sermon on the Mount when Jesus was encouraging His disciples to trust their Heavenly Father to meet their material needs, He said, *"Seek first the kingdom of God and His righteousness, and all these things shall be added to you"* (Matthew 6:33). As we are seeking to reflect the values of God's Kingdom in our personal life and family, we should also seek to bring those values to the world around us.

This is one of the central aspects of the prayer Jesus prescribed in Matthew 6:9-13: *"Your kingdom come. Your will be done on earth as it is in heaven."* In addition to being an important prayer for your individual life and your family, seeking more of God's Kingdom should be part of your prayer for your city and nation.

Can you imagine what your nation would be like if God's will was perfectly done there, just as it is in Heaven? In Heaven there is peace, contentment, holiness, joy, health, love, abundance—and so much more! There's no crime, addiction, sickness, or lack. As you pray and live your daily life, it should be your desire to bring more of this Heavenly realm to the world around you.

DISPENSING GOD'S PRESENCE EVERYWHERE

The Christians in the early church were able to turn the world upside down as they shared the Gospel of Jesus Christ everywhere they went. But an important key to their amazing impact was that people *"recognized that they had been with Jesus"* (Acts 4:13). In the same way, we'll only influence our world to the extent that we make it a priority to be *"with Jesus"* in daily worship, prayer, and intercession.

This same principle is seen in Mark 3:13-14, when Jesus appointed His 12 apostles *"that they might be **with Him** and that He might send them out to preach."* As Bible teacher and revivalist Leonard Ravenhill wrote several decades ago, "To be much FOR God, we must be much WITH God."

Today, just as the early church experienced, people will be able to *tell* if we've truly spent time with Jesus. As we regularly enter into His presence through thanksgiving, praise, and prayer (Psalm 100:4), we will be able to dispense that presence to a needy, sin-sick world:

> *Thanks be to God, who always leads us in triumph in Christ, and manifests through us the sweet aroma of the knowledge of Him in every place. For we are a fragrance of Christ to God among those who are*

being saved and among those who are perishing; to the one an aroma from death to death, to the other an aroma from life to life (2 Corinthians 2:14-16 NASB).

Your life of prayer and worship is the key to this kind of fragrant impact on your city and nation. The stench of sin and depravity can be dispelled by the aroma of Christ's presence emanating from your life.

Jesus died to restore us to our rightful relationship with the Father (John 14:6, 1 Peter 3:18), to atone for our sins (1 John 2:2), to give us back the keys to the Kingdom (Matthew 16:19), to restore our position of dominion on the earth (Genesis 1:26-28), and to make us Heaven's ambassadors in bringing God's Kingdom to earth (2 Corinthians 5:2).

Our mandate is to be part of filling the *whole earth* with God's glory—not just every Christian or every church. We're called to touch the kingdoms of this earth with the Kingdom of our Father in Heaven (Matthew 6:10, Revelation 11:15). That means impacting and influencing every sphere of society, including business, government, media, arts and entertainment, the family, and the church.

Yet too often we've allowed ourselves to be boxed in to a "stained glass ghetto." God's purpose is far bigger, though. He wants to fill the entire earth with His presence (Ephesians 4:10, Habakkuk 2:14).

Each of us is called to be a light, not just in the church, but also in some area of the marketplace. Scottish preacher George MacLeod pointed this out:

> I simply argue that the cross should be raised in the center of the marketplace as well as on the steeple of the church. I am recovering the claim that Jesus was not crucified between two candles, but on a cross between two thieves; on the town's garbage heap; at a crossroads, so cosmopolitan they had to write his title in Hebrew, in Latin, and in Greek. At the kind of place where cynics talk smut, and thieves curse, and soldiers gamble. Because that is where He died. That is what He died for. And that is what He died about. And that is where church

people ought to be, and what church people ought to be about.

As you intercede for your nation, make sure you have a vision to see the glory of the Lord fill every area of the culture, not just confined to the four walls of the church. Pray for an outpouring of His Spirit on your nation's spheres of business, government, media, arts and entertainment, education, family, and religion.

Trusting the King of Kings

Laying Hold of God's Promises

4

"Bear up the hands that hang down, by faith and prayer; support the tottering knees. Have you any days of fasting and prayer? Storm the throne of grace and persevere therein, and mercy will come down."

– John Wesley

When he was only 24 years old, Dwight L. Moody met a 73-year-old Methodist lay minister whose prayers ignited his entire being. It was as if Heaven came to earth each time this gentleman opened his mouth to pray. Determined to find out why, Moody approached the man and inquired as to his secret.

The man replied, "You've got to learn to pray

the promises of God." He had memorized as many of God's promises as his brain could hold, and his prayers were merely reminders to the Lord of what He had already promised to do.

There are nearly 8,000 promises in the Bible. Although there's no way you'll be able to memorize each and every one of them, your prayer life will dramatically improve if you can learn even a dozen or so.

Your Heavenly Father loves you! He wants to bless you, your loved ones, and your nation. He has made wonderful promises to you in His Word, and He wants you to hold Him to those promises when you pray.

Here are a few of God's promises to get you started:

1. God wants to answer your prayers.

"It shall come to pass that before they call I will answer; and while they are still speaking I will hear." – Isaiah 65:24

Not only does God promise to answer your prayers, but He even says He sends an answer before you're finished praying. He cares for you so tenderly that He knows what you are about to ask from Him and has already set in motion a plan to supply your need.

2. God wants people to come to repentance and a knowledge of the truth.

"The Lord is not slack concerning His promise, as some count slackness, but is longsuffering toward us, not willing that any should perish but that all should come to repentance." – 2 Peter 3:9

"This is good and acceptable in the sight of God our Savior, who desires all men to be saved and to come to the knowledge of the truth." – 1 Timothy 2:3-4

There was once a praying daughter who was claiming God's promises for the salvation of her father. He was tangled in the occult and dabbling in all sorts of dishonorable spiritual things that invite demonic activity. She faithfully prayed for him for 35 years, seemingly without effect. Finally, he neared the end of his days and was in a hospital room dying of heart failure at age 81.

"You need to place yourself in the hands of Jesus right now, Dad, before it's too late. Are you ready to do that?" she asked.

"Yes, yes, I am," he said with tears in his eyes.

After 35 years of continual prayer, this daughter's intercessory prayers were answered.

No matter how long it takes or how impossible the circumstances may seem, keep praying for the salvation of your loved ones and the restoration of your nation. Whether you can see it yet or not, the answer from God is on the way.

3. God cares about the world.

"God so loved the world that He gave His only begotten Son, that whoever believes in Him should not perish but have everlasting life. For God did not send His Son into the world to condemn the world, but that the world through Him might be saved." – John 3:16-17

Sometimes you might look at what is going on in the world, read troubling news articles or alarming posts on social media, and find it hard to believe that God would still be interested in saving and blessing people in this heartless world. Yet, because of His great love, Jesus left the grandeur of Heaven to come to earth in order *"to seek and to save that which was lost"* (Luke 19:10).

Instead of giving in to despair, we need to take heart—viewing the world through God's loving eyes and the redemption He provided in Christ. Even when we are tempted to give up and quit praying, the Lord will give us renewed hope. No matter how bleak our nation's condition may seem, we must continue to stand on His promises and proclaim them over our sin-sick, dying land.

STANDING IN THE GAP

During the days of the prophet Ezekiel, God said He was looking for someone to *"stand in the gap"* to avert His judgment on Jerusalem, but He *"found no one"*:

I looked for someone who might rebuild the wall of righteousness that guards the land. I searched for someone to stand in the gap in the wall so I wouldn't have to destroy the land, but I found no one (Ezekiel 22:30 NLT).

Jesus was the ultimate example of someone who stood in the gap, as He laid down His life to become the mediator between a holy God and sinful humanity (1 Timothy 2:5-6). But the Bible is filled with stories of other men and women who modeled a life of intercession or service for others. These include Abraham, Moses, Deborah, David, Abigail, Phineas, Esther, Nehemiah, Daniel, and Paul.

Daniel's prayer of intercession for his city and nation is particularly instructive about what it means to stand in the gap as we pray for others. Many Christians today are quick to point out the sins of their national leaders and their nation's culture, but their prayers are more like finger-pointing than genuine repentance. Daniel's prayer was much different. Although the Bible describes him as an exceptionally godly person, never mentioning any specific sins in his life, Daniel included himself in his prayer of repentance regarding the sins of his nation.

Take time to read this powerful prayer, applying it to yourself, your city, and your nation:

*Then I set my face toward the Lord God to make request by prayer and supplications, with fasting, sackcloth, and ashes. And I prayed to the L*ORD *my God, and made **confession**, and said, "O Lord, great and awesome God, who keeps His covenant and mercy with those who love Him, and with those who keep His commandments, **we have sinned and committed iniquity, we have done wickedly and rebelled, even by departing from Your precepts and Your judgments**. Neither have **we** heeded Your servants the prophets, who spoke in Your name to our kings and our princes, to our fathers and all the people of the land. O Lord, righteousness belongs to You, but **to us shame** of face…*

*O Lord, **to us belongs** shame of face, to our kings, our princes, and our fathers, because **we have sinned against You**. To the Lord our God belong mercy and* *forgiveness, though **we** have rebelled against Him. **We** have not obeyed the voice of the LORD our God, to walk in His laws, which He set before us by His servants the prophets. Yes, **all Israel has transgressed Your law**, and has departed so as not to obey Your voice; therefore the curse and the oath written in the Law of Moses the servant of God have been poured out on us, because **we** have sinned against Him. And He has confirmed His words, which He spoke against **us** and against our judges who judged us, by bringing upon **us** a great disaster; for under the whole heaven such has never been done as what has been done to Jerusalem.*

*As it is written in the Law of Moses, all this disaster has come upon **us**; yet **we have not made our prayer before the LORD our God, that we might turn from our iniquities and understand Your truth**. Therefore the LORD has kept the disaster in mind, and brought it upon **us**; for the LORD our God is righteous in all* *the works which He does, though **we have not obeyed His voice**. And now, O Lord our God, who brought Your people out of the land of Egypt with a mighty hand, and made Yourself a name, as it is this day— **we have sinned, we have done wickedly**!*

*O Lord, according to all Your righteousness, I pray, let Your anger and Your fury be turned away from Your city Jerusalem, Your holy mountain; because for **our sins**, and for the iniquities of our fathers, Jerusalem and Your people are a reproach to all those around **us**. Now therefore, our God, hear the prayer of Your servant, and his supplications, and for the Lord's sake cause Your face to shine on Your sanctuary, which is desolate. O my God, incline Your ear and hear; **open Your eyes and see our desolations**, and the city which is called by Your name; for **we** do not present **our** supplications before You because of **our** righteous deeds, but because of Your great mercies.*

O Lord, hear! O Lord, forgive! O Lord,

listen and act! Do not delay for Your own sake, my God, for Your city and Your people are called by Your name.

*Now while I was speaking, praying, and **confessing <u>my</u> sin and the sin of my people** Israel, and presenting my supplication before the LORD my God for the holy mountain of my God...* (Daniel 9:3-20).

Daniel could have prayed self-righteous prayers, asking God to bring repentance and restoration to others, while leaving himself off the hook. Remember the story Jesus told in Luke 18:9-14 about a man who prayed like that? He thanked God that he wasn't sinful like the people around him—*"extortioners, unjust, adulterers, or even as this tax collector"* (v. 11). This smug man went on to recite the religious things he had done to deserve right-standing with God: *"I fast twice a week; I give tithes of all that I possess"* (v. 12).

Meanwhile, a tax collector, despised by everyone, was also in the temple to pray that day. He took a far different approach, crying out for God's mercy instead of claiming entitlement based on his good works:

*The tax collector, standing afar off, would
not so much as raise his eyes to heaven,
but beat his breast, saying, "God, be
merciful to me a sinner!"* (v. 13).

Jesus concluded the story by warning us about the folly of approaching God in a prideful way:

*I tell you, this man went down to his
house justified rather than the other;
for everyone who exalts himself will be
humbled, and he who humbles himself
will be exalted* (v. 14).

Daniel was one of the righteous men of his generation, yet his intercession was based on God's mercy and faithfulness, rather than on his own merits and goodness.

WHERE ARE THE DANIELS TODAY?

The Lord is still looking for intercessors like Daniel to stand in the gap today. As we're told in 2 Chronicles 16:9 (NASB), *"The eyes of the Lord move to and fro throughout the earth that He may strongly support those whose heart is completely His."*

But this means humbling ourselves to identify with the sins of our nation, even if we haven't personally partaken in those sins. As Daniel did, we must confess our nation's sins as our *own.*

Another principle modeled throughout Daniel's prayer is that he focused on the Lord's character as the basis for his hope. For example, he pointed out that God is…

- Great and awesome
- A God who keeps His covenant
- Righteous
- A God of great mercy and forgiveness

In the same way, your petitions to God for your nation should be made on the basis of His character and compassion. Remind Him of what His Word says. Thank Him for His faithfulness to His promises.

As you join with other Believers in crying out to God for His mercy and forgiveness, He will hear from Heaven and begin to heal your land (2 Chronicles 7:14). As you repent on behalf of yourself, your nation, and your national leaders, you can unleash a spiritual awakening that will transform countless lives.

Laying Hold of God's Promises

PRAYING WITH AUTHORITY 5

*"More things are wrought by prayer
than this world dreams of."*
– Alfred, Lord Tennyson

How vast is Jesus' authority? Before His ascension, Jesus told His disciples, *"**All** authority has been given to Me in heaven and on earth"* (Matthew 28:18). Jesus doesn't share even one bit of His authority or glory with the devil! One day ***every*** knee will bow to Jesus, and ***every*** tongue will confess that He is Lord (Philippians 2:9-11).

The Bible says Jesus is seated at the Father's right hand, *"far **above all** principalities and power and might and dominion, and **every** name that is named, not only in this age but also in that which is* *to come. And He put **all things under His feet**, and gave Him to be **head over all things** to the church, which is His body, the fullness of Him who fills all in all"* (Ephesians 1:21-23). Since Jesus rules over all creation and rules over *us*, we have the right to exercise *His* authority against the powers of darkness when we pray for our city and nation.

However, today few Christians really grasp the awesome authority that belongs to them in Christ. A police officer can stand and direct traffic regardless of his physical stature, just because of the delegated authority he's received from the city or state. His badge of delegated authority is far more important than the officer's personal strength or power.

In the same way, Jesus has given us *His* badge of delegated authority. When we submit to Him and act in His name, all the power and resources of Heaven are at our disposal. No enemy can stand against us when we're truly submitted to Him (Romans 8:31). When we resist the devil and his minions, they must flee from us (James 4:7).

MOUNTAIN-MOVING FAITH

Many Christians acknowledge that *Jesus* has great authority, but they still can't grasp the fact that *His* authority is *their* authority! They go around discouraged and defeated, wondering why Jesus doesn't intervene in their circumstances. Yet the whole time, they have all the authority they need to "speak" to their circumstances in Jesus' mighty name: *"If you have faith as a mustard seed, you will say to this mountain, 'Move from here to there,' and it will move; and nothing will be impossible for you"* (Matthew 17:20).

Jesus prays to the Father in John 17:18, *"As You sent Me into the world, I also have sent them into the world."* God sent His Son to earth for a clear objective: *"For this purpose the Son of God was manifested, that He might destroy the works of the devil"* (1 John 3:8). The *"works of the devil"* are the consequences of sin that entered the world through the disobedience of Adam and Eve: such things as sin, sickness, relationship conflicts, and death.

Jesus was given *"all authority"* to accomplish His mission, and this same authority has now been given to *us*. Because He sent us in the same way that His Father sent Him, we have received *all* the authority that was delegated to Christ.

Yet Satan has intimidated many Christians into believing they are powerless against him. Perhaps you remember the scene from *The Wizard of Oz* movie when "the great and powerful Oz" was trying to terrify Dorothy and her friends. His fear tactics seemed to be succeeding until Dorothy's dog, Toto, pulled back the curtain. It turned out that the mighty Oz was actually just a feeble old man.

Don't let Satan scare you from praying bold, audacious prayers. Because you've been given the authority of Christ, there's no enemy that can stand against you when you pursue your destiny in His name.

BATTLING FOR YOUR PROMISED LAND

When you are battling in prayer for God's Kingdom to prevail in your nation, it's helpful to remember the lessons the Israelites learned when getting ready to fight for their Promised

Land. After the death of his mentor Moses, Joshua was given instructions from the Lord on how he could lead his people to victory:

1. Go on the offensive.

"Arise, go over this Jordan, you and all this people, to the land which I am giving to them —the children of Israel." – Joshua 1:2 NASB

In the same way, God's people will need to *ARISE* if they're going to reclaim their nation. That means getting out of our easy chairs and rousing yourselves for action. And just as Joshua and the Israelites had to **"go over"** the Jordan River, there are some things you'll need to *get over* and *overcome* in order to fulfill God's purposes.

2. Expand your vision.

"Every place that the sole of your foot will tread upon I have given you."
– Joshua 1:3 NASB

Remember what Psalm 24:1 declares: *"The earth is the LORD's, and all its fullness, the world and those who dwell therein."* This means the devil isn't the rightful owner of the earth or any of its inhabitants. God is the true owner, both through creation and through Christ's redemptive act on the cross, when He purchased back everything the enemy stole.

In his book, *City Reaching—On the Road to Community Transformation*, Jack Dennison points out, "The neighborhoods of your city belong to God. The cities of America belong to God. The nations of the world belong to God. He wants them, and He will have them—every one of them!"

Because our Lord is the rightful owner and ruler of every piece of ground and every person who inhabits our nation, we can have great boldness in our prayers and our witnessing. As long as we faithfully represent His Kingdom, God wants to give us dominion over every place our foot treads. We can be *victors* instead of *victims*.

3. Know your inheritance.

"From the wilderness and this Lebanon as far as the great river, the River Euphrates, all the land of the Hittites, and to the Great Sea toward the going down of the sun, shall be your territory." – Joshua 1:4 NASB

Each of us has been given specific *"territory"* in God's Kingdom. Joshua and the Israelites hadn't yet taken *any* of this territory, but God was letting them know it was His inheritance for them. Do you know what spiritual territory has been ordained for *you*? Perhaps there's a certain sphere of society where you are called to focus your prayers or outreach. For example, God may want you to be His ambassador to the world of business, government, media, arts and entertainment, education, or families.

4. Be confident of victory.

"No man shall be able to stand before you all the days of your life; as I was with Moses, so I will be with you. I will not leave you nor forsake you." – Joshua 1:5 NASB

Just think how bold we all would be if we knew that victory was certain and that God would never leave us. Instead of cowering in a corner, waiting for Jesus to come back and rescue us from the devil, we would be valiant warriors, continually taking more ground for the Kingdom of God.

5. Fight courageously.

"Be strong and of good courage, for to this people you shall divide as an inheritance the land which I swore to their fathers to give them. Only be strong and very courageous…Have I not commanded you? Be strong and of good courage; do not be afraid, nor be dismayed, for the LORD your God is with you wherever you go."
– Joshua 1:6-9 NASB

God knew the Promised Land would never be taken by pacifists. Still today, courage and strength are indispensable for spiritual progress and impact. A spiritual war is going on, and you can't afford to be a wimp!

THE VICTORY IS SURE

If spiritual battles are raging in your life, it's easy to forget an important truth: If our lives belong to Christ, our ultimate victory is certain.

Sure, there will be difficult battles and even setbacks along the way. At times it may seem as if the devil has gotten the upper hand. But when the final trumpet sounds, our Lord Jesus will overwhelmingly triumph. In fact, the victory song has already been written: *"Hallelujah! For the Lord our God, the Almighty, reigns!"* (Revelation 19:6).

Take courage in knowing you are on the winning team. The day will come when *"the earth will be filled with the knowledge of the glory of the Lord, as the waters cover the sea"* (Habakkuk 2:14).

Even while the battles continue, the future headline has been written in Revelation 11:15:

> ***The kingdoms of this world have become the kingdoms of our Lord and of His Christ, and He shall reign forever and ever!***

Remember: Demonic spirits and enemy strongholds are not invincible! Long before Jesus defeated sin, death, and Satan on the cross, God could look down through the corridors of time and see the certainty of our redemption—a day when the devil's head would be crushed. In Genesis 3:15, God tells the serpent, *"I will put enmity between you and the woman, and between your seed and her Seed; He shall bruise your head, and you shall bruise His heel."*

Paul refers to this in Romans 16:20 (NASB): *"The God of peace will soon crush Satan under your feet."* That's good news! In addition to interceding for your nation, perhaps you're battling the devil today for your health…your marriage…your children…your finances…or your emotional well-being. But soon—*very soon*—God has promised to crush Satan under your feet.

Praying with Authority

God's Formula to Heal Your Land

"Oh! men and brethren, what would this heart feel if I could but believe that there were some among you who would go home and pray for a revival: men whose faith is large enough, and their love fiery enough to lead them from this moment to exercise unceasing intercessions that God would appear among us and do wondrous things here, as in the times of former generations."
— Charles Spurgeon

If you were feeling sick and sought relief at a doctor's office, your physician would likely give you a prescription. "Here, take this and you'll get better," they might say.

In the same way, one of the names God calls Himself is *Jehovah Rapha*, which means He's "the

Lord your Healer or Doctor." And just like a human doctor, His treatment plan is only effective if you follow His instructions:

> *If you diligently heed the voice of the LORD your God and do what is right in His sight, give ear to His commandments and keep all His statutes, I will put none of the diseases on you which I have brought on the Egyptians* (Exodus 15:26).

In one of the clearest promises in God's Word, He gives us a precise formula or prescription for how healing and restoration can come to nation:

> *If My people who are called by My name will humble themselves, and pray and seek My face, and turn from their wicked ways, then I will hear from heaven, and will forgive their sin and heal their land* (2 Chronicles 7:14).

Each phrase of this beautiful promise is packed with meaning:

- **If My people who are called by My name...** Notice that the first step in national restoration is not that unbelievers repent.

God addresses His own people first, for that is where both judgment and mercy must begin (1 Peter 4:17-18). We who are called by the Lord's name must accept our responsibility to be His ambassadors to our sin-sick world (2 Corinthians 5:20).

- **Humble themselves, and pray and seek My face, and turn from their wicked ways...** Many preachers and many Christians today are experts on the *"wicked ways"* of the surrounding culture. We see all the ways our political leaders, celebrities, news organizations, and entertainment media need to repent. Yet that is not where God initially shines His spotlight. WE—those who claim to follow Jesus as our Savior and Lord—must first humble ourselves and turn from OUR wicked ways. We must go beyond "Now I Lay Me Down to Sleep" prayers and truly seek God's face.

- **THEN I will hear from heaven, and will forgive their sin and heal their land.** Notice that this phrase begins with *"then."* God wants us to see that although He wants to heal our land, His promise requires us to fulfill the *conditions* He has laid out. When we confess and acknowledge our sins, He will show us mercy and forgiveness (1 John 1:9).

HOPE FOR NATIONAL RESTORATION

Many nations are facing a tipping point today. Will we turn to God or continue our descent into spiritual darkness? Will the Lord give us wise and caring national leaders, or will we select leaders who openly reject Biblical precepts? Will He protect us from terrorism and natural disasters, or will we face an outpouring of His judgment?

As the people of God, the answer to these questions is in *our* hands. We can't just do the "same old, same old," and expect different results. There's still time to turn things around, but we can't afford to delay.

If your nation's moral trajectory has been on a downhill slide for many decades, you may be tempted to lose hope that change is possible. But the Bible gives us many illustrations of God's power to turn things around for a nation when His people turn to Him.

The book of Jonah tells the story of God's prophet being sent to the wicked Assyrian city of Nineveh. You've probably heard the story of Jonah's initial disobedience, which landed him in the belly of a huge fish for three days. Fortunately, God was merciful to Jonah, and he was given another chance to fulfill his mission. So if you feel like you're stuck in the belly of a fish today, take heart: *God wants to set you free and powerfully use you to transform lives!*

When Jonah finally got back on track and entered Nineveh, God gave him an ominous message to deliver: *"Forty days from now Nineveh will be destroyed!"* (Jonah 3:4 NLT).

Can you imagine being a Ninevite and hearing this sobering message? What would you do if God said He was going to destroy your city or nation within 40 days? How would you respond if you were warned that your life was in jeopardy—as well as the lives of your children and future generations?

Amazingly, Jonah's words brought about a

stunning revival: *"The people of Nineveh believed God, proclaimed a fast, and put on sackcloth, from the greatest to the least of them"* (v. 5). Even the king and his nobles joined in the repentance and cried out to God for His mercy: *"Who can tell if God will turn and relent, and turn away from His fierce anger, so that we may not perish?"* (v. 9).

What a hope-filled lesson for us today. The Lord was merciful to Nineveh when they repented, and He is willing to show mercy to your city and nation as well: *"Then God saw their works, that they turned from their evil way; and God relented from the disaster that He had said He would bring upon them, and He did not do it"* (v. 10).

Sadly, Jonah refused to rejoice when God spared Nineveh. Like the older brother in the Prodigal Son story (Luke 15:11-32), he wanted to see judgment poured out rather than mercy. Your nation may deserve God's judgment today, but you need to pray for repentance so it can receive His mercy instead.

AN OUTPOURING OF BLESSINGS

Instead of being destroyed in 40 days,

God's Formula to Heal Your Land

Nineveh repented and received God's mercy and healing. Wouldn't the same thing happen today if God's people took the next 40 days to humble themselves and cry out to Him as never before? And what would happen if you made a personal commitment to share this message with your friends and loved ones during the next 40 days, challenging them to intercede for your nation?

Rather than reaping judgment and curses, this can be a day of great blessing when we turn to the Lord and claim His promises in heartfelt prayer and fasting:

> *"Now, therefore," says the* LORD, *"Turn to Me with all your heart, with fasting, with weeping, and with mourning." So rend your heart, and not your garments; return to the* LORD YOUR GOD, *for He is gracious and merciful, slow to anger, and of great kindness; and He relents from doing harm. Who knows if He will turn and relent, and leave a blessing behind Him?* (Joel 2:12-14).

You don't need to be in any doubt: When you follow His prescription for revival and restoration,

God will *"leave a blessing"* for your nation.

WHY REVIVAL TARRIES

When God has given us such a clear formula for igniting a revival, it may seem strange that true revivals are a fairly rare occurrence. In 1959, Leonard Ravenhill wrote a classic book called *Why Revival Tarries*. He described some reasons why the church doesn't often see revival:

> We're content to live without it. It's too costly. We don't want God to disrupt our status quo. The Christian life can only be lived one way, and that's God's way. And God's way is that I leave all and follow Him…When I think I've "arrived" at something, the Lord shutters that.

In many ways, a revival is certainly a supernatural occurrence—a miracle from God. But several of history's greatest revivalists have pointed out that spiritual awakenings don't just happen randomly or by accident. Rather than being caused by some kind of mystery, revivals are the result of God's people following Biblical principles:

> A revival is no more a miracle than a crop of wheat. In any community, revival can be secured from Heaven when heroic souls enter the conflict determined to win or die—or if need be, to win *and* die!
> – John Wesley

> A revival can be *expected* when Christians have a spirit of prayer for revival. – Charles Finney

> The carpet in front of the mirrors in some of you people is worn threadbare, while at the side of your bed where you should kneel in prayer is as good as the day you put it down. – Billy Sunday

The point is this: When we follow God's prescription for revival, it will surely come. We may need some perseverance in our prayers, but the Lord will surely answer if we meet His conditions.

A SIMPLE PATTERN

Revivals and spiritual awakenings throughout history have ordinarily followed a predictable

Biblical pattern:

- God's people see their need and beginning to earnestly pray.
- As they enter deeper into His presence, they begin to get honest with Him and with each other.
- This honesty brings them to a place of repentance before God, and then confession and reconciliation with each other.
- Their repentance leads to a new commitment to obey God and a new level of unity with other Believers.
- This renewed obedience and unity leads to true worship of the Lord and then powerful outreach to the Lost.
- When these factors all come together, REVIVAL has begun!

This chart shows the progression of indispensable steps toward a genuine revival or spiritual awakening, along with Bible references:

God's Formula to Heal Your Land

PRAYER

The starting point, breaking up the fallow ground (Hosea 10:12).

2 Chronicles 7:14, Isaiah 64:1, Psalm 68:1,
Psalm 85:6, Psalm 119:25, Habakkuk 3:2,
Hosea 6:1-3, Acts chapters 1, 2, 3, 4, etc.

YOUR RELATIONSHIP WITH GOD	YOUR RELATIONSHIP WITH PEOPLE
Honesty with God Isaiah 6:1-9	**Honesty with Others** 1 John 1:7
Repentance (humility toward God) 1 John 1:8-10, Acts 3:19-21	**Reconciled with Others** Matthew 5:23-24, John 17:21-23, John 13:34-25
Obedience Luke 6:46 John 14:15, John 14:21	**Unity with Believers** Acts 4:23-37, John 13:24-25, John 17:21-23
True Worship Acts 2:47, Matthew 28:18-20	**Outreach to the Lost** Matthew 9:36-38, Isaiah 6:8-9

REVIVAL!

WILL *YOU* FOLLOW THE FORMULA?

Just as a prescription from your doctor will do you no good unless you actually follow his instructions and take the medicine, this chart on revival works the same way. Unless you take time to humble yourself before the Lord and apply these Biblical principles.

We live in an hour of great urgency for a spiritual awakening in the nations of the world, so there's no time to procrastinate. The best time to get start praying for revival in your nation is *today*.

God's Formula to Heal Your Land

Is God on Your Nation's Side?

7

"O that we were more deeply moved by the languishing state of Christ's cause upon the earth today, by the inroads of the enemy and the awful desolation he has wrought. Alas that a spirit of indifference, or at least of fatalistic stoicism, is freezing so many of us."
– A.W. Pink

For an individual or a nation, nothing is more important than the favor of God. If we have His favor, we can be confident all things will work together for our good (Romans 8:28). When we live under the canopy of God's covenant, He gives us *"power to get wealth"* and many other blessings (Deuteronomy 8:18, Deuteronomy 28:1-14).

Romans 8:31 asks, *"If God is for us, who can*

be against us?" That means we have nothing to fear from our enemies. With the Lord on our side, there's no foe too big, too powerful, or too crafty. When we walk in His victory procession, we can triumph in every situation (2 Corinthians 2:14).

King David understood this. That's why he could be so confident when he faced nine-foot-tall Goliath with just a slingshot and five smooth stones (1 Samuel 17).

But in Psalm 124 David showed that he *also* recognized the flip side of this truth: If God was *not* on the side of the Israelites, they would have been swallowed up by their enemies (v. 3) and drowned in the flood waters of life (v. 4). He knew that the only thing protecting the Israelites was the favor of God.

David concluded this psalm by giving the Lord full credit for Israel's blessings: *"Our help is in the name of the Lord, who made heaven and earth"* (v. 8). Let those words sink in for a moment. If the one *"who made heaven and earth"* is truly your Helper and the Helper of your nation, you have absolutely nothing to fear.

Is God on Your Nation's Side?

"*IF* GOD IS FOR US..."

However, Romans 8:31 doesn't promise that God will *automatically* be on your side or your nation's side. The verse begins with a big *"IF..."* It's only *"if"* God is for us that we can be assured of success and victory.

So how can we really be *sure* that God is truly for us and for our nation? It's presumptuous to think a nation will always have God's favor, just because of its past Christian heritage. Yet many people think that way. "Of course God is on our side!" they confidently say. "Over the centuries, we've had a rich history of godly leaders, revivals, and missionaries. Certainly the Lord will back us in the battles we face today."

Not so fast. Many of the same chapters that promise God's covenant blessings when we obey Him also warn that His blessings will be withdrawn if we turn our back on Him (for example, Deuteronomy 8:18-20 and 28:15-68).

American President Abraham Lincoln, like King David, recognized nations are only blessed to the fullest extent when their God is the Lord. He warned that nations must not presumptuously think they will continue to experience God's blessings, despite their pride and disobedience:

> We have been the recipients of the choicest bounties of Heaven. We have been preserved, these many years, in peace and prosperity. We have grown in numbers, wealth and power, as no other nation has ever grown. But we have forgotten God. We have forgotten the gracious hand which preserved us in peace, and multiplied and enriched and strengthened us; and we have vainly imagined, in the deceitfulness of our hearts, that all these blessings were produced by some superior wisdom and virtue of our own. Intoxicated with unbroken success, we have become too self-sufficient to feel the necessity of redeeming and preserving grace, too proud to pray to the God that made us!
>
> It behooves us then, to humble ourselves before the offended Power, to

confess our national sins, and to pray for clemency and forgiveness...

(Presidential Proclamation *"Appointing a Day of National Humiliation, Fasting, and Prayer,"* March 30, 1863).

WHOSE SIDE ARE YOU ON?

Shortly before Joshua would lead the Israelites in a battle against Jericho, he had a highly unusual encounter with a mighty angel of God:

He lifted his eyes and looked, and behold, a Man stood opposite him with His sword drawn in His hand. And Joshua went to Him and said to Him, "Are You for us or for our adversaries?" (Joshua 5:13).

Joshua recognized that this was a very important question. If this powerful angel was going to fight on his side, he had nothing to fear. But there was going to be big trouble if the angel had come to support Israel's adversaries.

Nevertheless, this may seem like a

strange question in some ways. Couldn't Joshua have safely assumed the angel of the Lord would be on Israel's side rather than supporting their pagan enemies?

Surprisingly, the angel didn't really answer Joshua's question. Joshua was seeking assurance that the angel armies had shown up to support the Israelites, and his question asked for a simple reply: Are you with US or THEM?

However, the angel said, "No, but as Commander of the army of the LORD I have now come" (v. 14).

This is a sobering story if you are seeking confirmation that God is on your nation's side today. The answer to Joshua's question boiled down to this: The angelic army was there to support the purposes of God. If the Israelites aligned themselves with those purposes, Heaven's army would come to their aid. But if they didn't submit to the Lord's plans, they couldn't expect His help.

Realizing that he better immediately surrender to God's messenger if he wanted to be assured of success and victory, *"Joshua fell on his face to the earth and worshiped, and said to Him, 'What does my Lord say to His servant?'"* (v. 14). Notice that he didn't just ask for victory—he asked for *divine instructions* for how to proceed.

YOUR NATION'S CHOICE

Joshua learned a powerful lesson when the angel appeared to him before the battle for Jericho: If we want God to be on OUR side, we must be sure we are on HIS side. So it's foolish for a country to continually disregard God's moral precepts but then seek His aid in times of war or crisis.

At the end of Joshua's life, he challenged the Israelites about their need to make a firm, deliberate, personal choice for themselves and their families:

Choose for yourselves this day whom you will serve, whether the gods which your fathers served that were on the other side of the River, or the gods of the Amorites, in whose land you dwell. But as for me and *my house, we will serve the L*ORD (Joshua 24:15 NASB).

Joshua was speaking to people who had a clear *heritage* with the God of Israel, but not necessarily a true *personal allegiance*. He wanted them to understand that the Lord would never be satisfied with a half-hearted, compromised commitment.

These words of Joshua could well be addressed to many professing Christians today. Perhaps they grew up in the Christian tradition, with parents or grandparents who were genuine Believers. But, too often, such people have become "secondhand saints," relying on their Christian heritage but not cultivating a personal relationship with God.

Joshua's statement about the need to *"choose"* was a candid recognition that people have many other "gods" they can follow instead of the Lord. In fact, *anything* we love or serve more than we love God has become an idol in our lives. And the Bible even warns us not to become *"lovers of pleasure rather than lovers of God"* (2 Timothy 3:4).

Joshua's exhortation was a challenge to those who want it "both ways"—serving the Lord when it's convenient, but keeping the option open to serve other gods as well. But he wasn't the least bit wishy-washy about which side he and his family were on: *"As for me and my house, we will serve the LORD"* (Joshua 24:15).

As you're praying for your nation, make sure you've made this same kind of clear and unequivocal commitment to the lordship of Jesus Christ. That's the only way your prayers will be effective in gaining victory over the devil's strongholds in your country.

CHOICES AND CONSEQUENCES

It's not surprising that this matter of choice was such a touchy issue with Joshua. Throughout his life, he had witnessed painful examples of people making wrong choices:

- The Israelites allowed fear and unbelief to keep them out of the Promised Land, and their cowardly decision resulted in 40 years of wandering in the wilderness (Numbers 13:1-14:24).

- By failing to obey the Lord in *speaking* to the rock rather than *striking* it, Joshua's mentor, Moses, was prohibited from entering the Promised Land (Numbers 20:9-12).

- Achan's decision to disobey the Lord and keep some of the plunder from Jericho resulted in his death, his children's death, and Israel's initial defeat at Ai (Joshua 7:1-26).

- By failing to seek the counsel of the Lord, the Israelites unwittingly were fooled into making a treaty with their enemy, the Gibeonites (Joshua 9:3-27).

Joshua saw how serious our choices are, whether individually or as a nation. These decisions inevitably determine our consequences… our rewards…and our destiny.

Joshua's passionate appeal for people to *"choose"* whom they would serve was an echo of God's earlier challenge in Deuteronomy 30:15-20 (NASB):

See, I have set before you today life and prosperity, and death and adversity; in that I command you today to love the Lord *your God, to walk in His ways*

*and to keep His commandments and His
statutes and His judgments, that you may
live and multiply, and that the LORD your
God may bless you in the land where you
are entering to possess it. But if your heart
turns away and you will not obey, but are
drawn away and worship other gods and
serve them, I declare to you today that you
shall surely perish. You will not prolong
your days in the land where you are crossing the Jordan to enter and possess it.*

*I call heaven and earth to witness against
you today, that I have set before you life
and death, the blessing and the curse. So
choose life in order that you may live, you
and your descendants, by loving the LORD
your God, by obeying His voice, and by
holding fast to Him; for this is your life
and the length of your days...*

God offers your nation this same sobering choice today—a choice that will affect its destiny. Based on the decisions its citizens make, your country can experience life or death…the blessing or the curse. And in case people aren't quite sure which choice to make, God makes it totally clear: *"CHOOSE LIFE."*

As you intercede for your nation, don't miss this important fact: Spiritual victory and blessing aren't automatic, but must be actively and aggressively *chosen*. There's no neutral ground! If a nation turns its back on the Lord and His ways, it has chosen the path of curses instead of blessings.

TURNING FROM IDOLS TO GOD

Even after the days of Joshua, "decision" continued to be an important theme of God's words to His people. The Lord repeatedly sent His messengers to challenge those who thought they could postpone or avoid making a firm decision to either obey or rebel. The prophetic message has always been clear: It's time to get off the fence and take a stand!

The world clearly has squeezed many lukewarm Believers into its mold (Romans 12:2). Instead of reflecting the values and lifestyle of the Kingdom of Heaven, we too often are merely reflecting the humanistic standards of the surrounding culture. Much of this compromise and half-heartedness is the result of our failure to make a clear decision to submit to God and resist the devil.

In contrast, those who heard the powerful Gospel message proclaimed by the early church *"turned to God from idols to serve the living and true God"* (1 Thessalonians 1:9 NASB). This kind of response brings genuine transformation to people's lives, just as it did when Paul brought the Gospel to Ephesus:

> *Many who had believed came confessing and telling their deeds. Also, many of those who had practiced magic brought their books together and burned them in the sight of all. And they counted up the value of them, and it totaled fifty thousand pieces of silver. So the word of the Lord grew mightily and prevailed* (Acts 19:18-20 NASB).

The conclusion of this passage says God's Word *"grew mightily and prevailed."* But look at the preceding steps that made such a move of God possible:

1. **Confession** – They were willing to openly admit the idolatry that had bound them.
2. **Cutting all ties** – They took immediate action to burn and destroy any possessions that had been connected to their idolatry. They literally "burned their bridges" back to the enemy's snares.
3. **Paying the price** – This definitely wasn't "easy believe-ism," for it cost them dearly to forsake their idols.

If you want to see fresh breakthroughs from God in your life, look over these three responses again. Make sure you've totally cut off any ties with idolatry to false gods.

THE VALLEY OF DECISION

The prophet Elijah was grieved that many people of his day refused to make a clear decision for the Lord. They wanted it both ways, claiming to serve the Lord, but at the same time worshiping false gods such as Baal and the Asherah.

Elijah confronted them with a call for decision: *"How long will you hesitate between two opinions? If the LORD is God, follow Him; but if Baal, follow him*" (1 Kings 18:21 NASB). Elijah put the choice in very clear terms. There was no time for delay, nor any room for neutrality or "middle ground."

Sadly, the Israelites were still not ready to decide: *"The people did not answer him a word."* Instead of seeing the error of their ways and immediately repenting, they waited until Elijah called down fire from Heaven in a "power encounter" with the prophets of Baal.

After fire came down from the sky and consumed Elijah's sacrifice on the altar, the people finally reached their long-awaited verdict: *"When all the people saw it, they fell on their faces; and they said, 'The LORD, He is God; the LORD, He is God'"* (1 Kings 18:39 NASB).

Perhaps your nation has been like the Israelites, prone to *"hesitate between two opinions."* What more can the Lord do to prove Himself? Does fire have to fall from the sky before people give themselves fully to Him?

Joel 3:14 provides an apt description of the

nations of the world today: *"Multitudes, multitudes in the valley of decision! For the day of the Lord is near in the valley of decision."* God is challenging people in your nation—and every nation—to repent from procrastination and compromise, heeding the words of Joshua: *"**Choose** for yourselves **this day** whom you will serve"* (Joshua 24:15).

Pray that people in your nation will heed God's prophetic cry today. It's time for everyone to choose which side they're on—and then live a life that reflects that allegiance.

Is God on Your Nation's Side?

When Light Breaks Through the Darkness

8

*"The church on its knees would bring
Heaven upon the earth."*
– E.M. Bounds

We shouldn't be surprised that we live in a time when there is much spiritual darkness across the earth. Long ago, the Apostle Paul wrote:

Know this, that in the last days perilous times will come: For men will be lovers of themselves, lovers of money, boasters, proud, blasphemers, disobedient to parents, unthankful, unholy, unloving, unforgiving, slanderers, without self-control, brutal, despisers of good, traitors, headstrong, haughty, lovers of pleasure rather than lovers of God, having a form of godliness but denying its power. And from such people turn away! For of this sort are those who creep into households and make captives of gullible women loaded down with sins, led away by various lusts, always learning and never able to come to the knowledge of the truth (2 Timothy 3:1-7).

Yet the Bible also gives us reason for much hope:

Arise, shine; For your light has come! And the glory of the Lord is risen upon you. For behold, the darkness shall cover the earth, And deep darkness the people; But the Lord will arise over you, And His glory will be seen upon you (Isaiah 60:1-2).

Look at the contrast the prophet Isaiah is describing here. On the hand, he says there will come a day of *"deep darkness."* But rather than being a cause for despair, he says this will be a time of *opportunity*. It will be a day for the people of God to arise and shine, reflecting His light and glory as never before.

In the following chapter, Isaiah continues this theme of awakening, restoration, and healing:

> *The Spirit of the Lord GOD is upon Me,*
> *Because the LORD has anointed Me*
> *To preach good tidings to the poor;*
> *He has sent Me to heal the brokenhearted,*
> *To proclaim liberty to the captives,*
> *And the opening of the prison to those who*
>   *are bound;*
> *To proclaim the acceptable year of the LORD,*
> *And the day of vengeance of our God;*
> *To comfort all who mourn,*
> *To console those who mourn in Zion,*
> *To give them beauty for ashes,*
> *The oil of joy for mourning,*
> *The garment of praise for the spirit of heaviness;*
> *That they may be called trees of righteousness,*
> *The planting of the LORD, that He may be*
>   *glorified* (Isaiah 61:1-3).

Jesus said this prophecy was fulfilled in His life and ministry (Luke 4:16-21). But it is *also* a picture of what happens when the fullness of the Holy Spirit is poured out on the church. When we intercede for our nation, we must also intercede for the church of Jesus Christ to rise up and demonstrate His supernatural ministry to a needy world. When spiritual awakening comes to God's people in our nation, we will…

- Preach good news to the poor.
- Heal the brokenhearted.
- Proclaim liberty to spiritual captives and prisoners of the enemy.
- Declare the availability of God's favor to all who come to Him.
- Comfort those who mourn.
- Show people how they can exchange their ashes and devastation for beauty and joy.

Isaiah says this Spirit-empowered ministry will not just impact individuals, but entire communities, cities, and nations:

And they shall rebuild the old ruins,
They shall raise up the former desolations,
And they shall repair the ruined cities,
The desolations of many generations (v. 4).

Today many of the foundations of civilization are in ruins, needing to be rebuilt. In some cases, the deterioration has gone on for *"many generations,"* but even then, this prophecy says there is hope. Even the *"ruined cities"* can be repaired when the Holy Spirit is poured out afresh on the people of God!

PRAYERS FOR SPECIFIC PURPOSES 9

"No one is greater than his prayer life. The pastor who is not praying is playing; the people who are not praying are straying. We have many organizers, but few agonizers; many players and payers, few pray-ers; many singers, few clingers; lots of pastors, few wrestlers; many fears, few tears; much fashion, little passion; many interferers, few intercessors; many writers, but few fighters. Failing here, we fail everywhere."
— Leonard Ravenhill

PRAYERS OF FORGIVENESS

"If we confess our sins, He is faithful and just to forgive our sins and to cleanse us from all unrighteousness." – 1 John 1:9

God promises both to *forgive* and to *cleanse*

us. The blood of Jesus not only deals with *some* sins, but rather it covers *"ALL unrighteousness."* That's why we're told in Romans 8:1, *"There is therefore now no condemnation to those who are in Christ Jesus."*

Yet the flip side of the forgiveness issue is that the Bible repeatedly tells us we must *forgive others* as the Lord has forgiven us (Matthew 6:12, Ephesians 4:32, Colossians 3:12-15).

Both of these aspects of forgiveness are crucial for your success as an intercessor. First, you must recognize—deep in your heart—that God loves you and has forgiven you in Christ, making you *"the righteousness of God"* in Him (2 Corinthians 5:21). But it is also necessary for you to extend forgiveness to anyone who has wronged you—potentially including even those like your national or city leaders (people you've never met, but nevertheless must forgive).

PRAYERS OF FAITH

"If any of you lacks wisdom, let him ask of God, who gives to all liberally and without reproach, and it will be given to him. But

Prayers for Specific Purposes

let him ask in faith, with no doubting, for he who doubts is like a wave of the sea driven and tossed by the wind. For let not that man suppose that he will receive anything from the Lord; he is a double-minded man, unstable in all his ways" – James 1:5-8

Prayers do no good unless they are prayers of faith. Otherwise, as James says, we are being *"double-minded"* and can't expect to receive anything from the Lord.

Faith is the substance of things hoped for, the very essence of all the unseen things we long to receive from God (Hebrews 11:1). And Hebrews 11:6 says, *"Without faith it is impossible to please Him, for he who comes to God must believe that He is, and that He is a rewarder of those who diligently seek Him."*

When you pray for your nation, cast aside your doubts and unbelief. Instead of focusing on the circumstances, fix your eyes on Jesus, *"the author and finisher of our faith"* (Hebrews 12:2). You can have faith in your faithful God!

PRAYERS OF HUMILITY AND CONTRITION

"On this one will I look: On him who is poor and of a contrite spirit, and who trembles at My word." – Isaiah 66:2

In this world system, power often seems to be in the hands of the rich and famous. But in God's Kingdom, He resists the proud and gives grace to the humble (1 Peter 5:5-6). Those who tremble at His Word—committed to obedience—receive His favor.

PRAYERS OF REPENTANCE

"Have mercy upon me, O God, according to Your lovingkindness; according to the multitude of Your tender mercies, blot out my transgressions…Wash me thoroughly from my iniquity, and cleanse me from my sin. For I acknowledge my transgressions, and my sin is always before me. Against You, You only, have I sinned, and done this evil in Your sight—that You may be found just when You speak, and blameless when You judge." – Psalm 51:1-4

Psalm 51 is David's prayer of repentance after his sin with Bathsheba was exposed. Not only did David humbly seek God's forgiveness, but he also recognized his need for the Lord to restore him to a clean heart…a steadfast spirit…a new sense of God's presence…and the joy of his salvation (vs. 10-12). While King Saul often tried to rationalize and minimize the importance of his sins and disobedience, David took full responsibility.

ADDING FASTING TO YOUR PRAYERS

"Is this not the fast that I have chosen: to loose the bonds of wickedness, to undo the heavy burdens, to let the oppressed go free, and that you break every yoke?"
– Isaiah 58:6

While you are interceding for your nation, you may be called upon to fast for a time over a specific prayer request. If you believe God is requiring that of you, respond to Him with humility and ask Him to help you.

Fasting can bring extra power and strength to your intercessory prayers as many authors have noted:

"Prayer is reaching out and after the unseen; fasting, letting go of all that is seen and temporal. Fasting helps express, deepens, confirms the resolution that we are ready to sacrifice anything, even ourselves, to attain, what we seek for the kingdom of God." – Andrew Murray

"Fasting confirms our utter dependence upon God by finding in Him a source of sustenance beyond food."
– Dallas Willard

"When exercised with a pure heart and a right motive, fasting may provide us with a key to unlock doors where other keys have failed; a window opening up new horizons in the unseen world; a spiritual weapon of God's provision, mighty, to the pulling down of strongholds." – Arthur Wallis

God often responds with miraculous wonders when we combine prayer and fasting. He releases people from bondage to sin, heals them, restores them, and prospers them. Sometimes the enemy onslaught seems overwhelming, especially in nations where evil abounds and wickedness in high places opens them up to demonic activity. But if God is calling you to fast, you can be confident He intends to break chains, unlock prison doors, and set captives free.

Isaiah 58 describes how Believers can unleash more of God's power in their lives by acknowledging their sins and returning to Him with repentance, prayer, and fasting. The chapter also describes how amazing blessings can be released when we care for the poor and share our bread with the hungry: *"Then your light shall break forth like the morning, your healing shall spring forth speedily, and your righteousness shall go before you; the glory of the LORD shall be your rear guard"* (vs. 7-8).

In addition, God promises us a new level of answered prayer and spiritual impact: *"Then you shall call, and the LORD will answer; you shall cry, and He will say, 'Here I am'…Then your light shall dawn in the darkness, and your darkness shall be as the noonday"* (v. 9). The result can be a new dimension of God's guidance, provision, and strength: *"The LORD will guide you continually, and satisfy your soul in drought, and strengthen your bones; you shall be like a watered garden, and like a spring of water, whose waters do not fail"* (v. 11).

The chapter ends with this promise when we delight ourselves in the Lord: *"I will cause you to ride on the high hills of the earth, and feed you with the heritage of Jacob your father"* (v. 14). When He becomes your delight, He will lift you up. His light…His glory…His favor…and His healing power will spring forth in greater magnitude than you've ever experienced before. This is the amazing, supernatural life God wants to give you as you draw near to Him with prayer and fasting.

You can read more about fasting in books of the Bible like Esther, Daniel, Jonah, Joel, Ezra, Nehemiah, the Gospels, and Acts. In addition to the benefits of fasting an individual can receive, several of the passages show the connection corporate fasting can have in restoring God's blessings to a city or nation.

PRAYERS THAT THWART THE ACCUSER

"Now salvation, and strength, and the kingdom of our God, and the power of His

Christ have come, for the accuser of our brethren, who accused them before our God day and night, has been cast down."
– Revelation 12:10

Satan is both a liar and an accuser. He does his best to bring feelings of guilt, condemnation, and shame upon even those who have been redeemed by Jesus Christ. How can these attacks be overcome? Revelation 12:11 tells us clearly: *"They overcame him by the blood of the Lamb and by the word of their testimony, and they did not love their lives to the death."*

When the accuser arises against you, your loved ones, or your nation, you need to apply *"the blood of the Lamb,"* reminding the devil that you have received forgiveness and justification in Christ. Speak bold prayers, testifying of what Jesus has done to set you free.

PRAYING AGAINST PRINCIPALITIES AND POWERS

"We do not wrestle against flesh and blood, but against principalities, against powers, against the rulers of the darkness of this

age, against spiritual hosts of wickedness in the heavenly places." – Ephesians 6:12

When you come against demonic strongholds and principalities, it's vital that you come to the battle clothed in *"the full armor of God,"* equipped with *"the sword of the Spirit, which is the word of God"* (Ephesians 6:10-18). Like Jesus did in Luke 4:1-13, proclaim the promises of Scripture when you face the enemy. God's Word can set people free from poverty, sickness, perversion, addiction, shame, or any of the devil's other traps.

Second Corinthians 10:4-5 assures us that *"the weapons of our warfare are not carnal but mighty in God for pulling down strongholds, casting down arguments and every high thing that exalts itself against the knowledge of God."* Jesus has already defeated the enemy (Colossians 2:15, 1 Peter 3:22), and He has given you everything you need to walk in His victory! *"No weapon forged against you will prevail, and you will refute every tongue that accuses you"* (Isaiah 54:17 NIV).

PRAYERS THAT UNMASK SATAN'S SCHEMES

"...so that no advantage would be taken of us by Satan, for we are not ignorant of his schemes." – 2 Corinthians 2:11 NASB

Jesus described Satan as *"a liar and the father of lies"* (John 8:44 NASB). To unmask him, you need to know God's Word and know the voice of the Holy Spirit. We live in a relativistic world where many people would rather do whatever is right in their own eyes instead of seek for God's truth (Judges 21:25). Our only hope is to allow the plumb line of truth to show us right from wrong, exposing the devil's lies in the process (Isaiah 28:17, Amos 7:7-8, Zechariah 4:10).

God wants to show mercy to your nation, but the Bible often shows a close association of mercy with truth: *"All the paths of the Lord are mercy and truth, to such as keep His covenant and His testimonies"* (Psalm 25:10; also see Psalm 57:3, 57:10, 85:10). When we embrace the Lord's truth, we receive His mercy as well. And as Jesus said in John 8:32, the truth has power to set us free.

PRAYERS FOR PROTECTION

"The eternal God is your refuge, and underneath are the everlasting arms; He will thrust out the enemy from before you, and will say, 'Destroy!'" – Deuteronomy 33:27

Jesus has already triumphed over the powers of darkness. When we need protection from the enemy, we can go to the Lord and ask for it, with full assurance that He will help us. When we put our trust in Him, the armies of Heaven are available for our protection and the protection of our nation.

As intercessors for our nations, we're in a dangerous war zone. Yet in Psalm 91:1-16 God promises us His protection:

*He who dwells in the secret place of the Most High shall abide under the shadow of the Almighty. I will say of the L*ORD*, "He is my refuge and my fortress; my God, in Him I will trust."*

Surely He shall deliver you from the snare of the fowler and from the perilous pestilence.

Prayers for Specific Purposes

He shall cover you with His feathers, and under His wings you shall take refuge; His truth shall be your shield and buckler. You shall not be afraid of the terror by night, nor of the arrow that flies by day, nor of the pestilence that walks in darkness, nor of the destruction that lays waste at noonday.

A thousand may fall at your side, and ten thousand at your right hand; but it shall not come near you. Only with your eyes shall you look, and see the reward of the wicked.

Because you have made the LORD, who is my refuge, even the Most High, your dwelling place, no evil shall befall you, nor shall any plague come near your dwelling; for He shall give His angels charge over you, to keep you in all your ways In their hands they shall bear you up, lest you dash your foot against a stone. You shall tread upon the lion and the cobra, the young lion and the serpent you shall trample underfoot.

"Because he has set his love upon Me, therefore I will deliver him; I will set him on

high, because he has known My name. He shall call upon Me, and I will answer him; I will be with him in trouble; I will deliver him and honor him. With long life I will satisfy him, and show him My salvation."

No matter how fierce the battle may become, you can trust in the Lord to keep you safe. When you obey His instructions, He promises to be "*an enemy to your enemies and an adversary to your adversaries*" (Exodus 23:22).

CALLING THE LOST OUT OF DARKNESS

"He brought them out of darkness and the shadow of death, and broke their chains in pieces." – Psalm 107:14

The very best way to transform your nation is for lost people to be saved—*"delivered… from the domain of darkness and transferred… to the kingdom of his beloved Son"* (Colossians 1:13 ESV). Your prayers can play a major role in this, asking the Lord *"to open their eyes, in order to turn them from darkness to light, and from the power of Satan to God, that they may re-*

ceive forgiveness of sins and an inheritance among those who are sanctified by faith" (Acts 26:18).

God has already done this for us, and now He wants us to be His instruments in praying for and witnessing to others. *"It is the God who commanded light to shine out of darkness, who has shone in our hearts to give the light of the knowledge of the glory of God in the face of Jesus Christ"* (2 Corinthians 4:6).

So go ahead and pray for the Lost, calling them out of darkness. Pray daily that the light of Jesus Christ will penetrate all darkness in their hearts so they can come to Him and be saved.

RECOGNIZING UNMET NEEDS

> *"Pure and undefiled religion before God and the Father is this: to visit orphans and widows in their trouble."* – James 1:27

When we're devoted to praying for our nation to experience a spiritual awakening, it can be easy to forget an important point: Sometimes our prayers must have hands and feet connected to them. This principle is found throughout the

Bible. For example, Psalm 82:3 says, *"Defend the poor and fatherless; do justice to the afflicted and needy."* It doesn't just say to *pray* for needy people—it says to *help* them!

The Apostle John wrote, *"By this we know love, because He laid down His life for us. And we also ought to lay down our lives for the brethren. But whoever has this world's goods, and sees his brother in need, and shuts up his heart from him, how does the love of God abide in him? My little children, let us not love in word or in tongue, but in deed and in truth"* (1 John 3:16-18).

And James adds, *"If a brother or sister is naked and destitute of daily food, and one of you says to them, 'Depart in peace, be warmed and filled,' but you do not give them the things which are needed for the body, what does it profit? Thus also faith by itself, if it does not have works, is dead"* (James 2:15-17).

So as you pray for your city and nation, ask the Lord if there's anything you can do to help the needy people around you. You can be the fragrance of Christ to your community and the hands and feet of Jesus to the least and the Lost. Is there a food bank in your city you can assist? Are there unwed mothers who need to see the compassion of Jesus in their difficult situation? Have refugees come into your country, needing someone to supply them with food, diapers, blankets, and winter coats? Let God lead you by His Spirit to where you can make the most impact.

PRAYING WHEN YOU DON'T KNOW WHAT TO PRAY

"The Spirit also helps in our weaknesses. For we do not know what we should pray for as we ought, but the Spirit Himself makes intercession for us with groanings which cannot be uttered. Now He who searches the hearts knows what the mind of the Spirit is, because He makes intercession for the saints according to the will of God." – Romans 8:26-27

Sometimes your burden to pray for your nation may become so deep that you feel as if there are no words to speak. The needs are simply too overwhelming, too bewildering. You may even find yourself groaning, much like a woman labors while giving birth. At times like that, God wants you to know that He values your birth pangs as you intercede. In the verse above, Paul writes that the Holy Spirit will help you in those times of weakness and travail. The Spirit will intercede through you *"according to the will of God."*

PRAYERS FOR STRENGTH AND ENDURANCE

"You have need of endurance, so that after you have done the will of God, you may receive the promise." – Hebrews 10:36

Praying for a spiritual awakening in your nation can often seem like an arduous, exhausting task. Too often, God's people lose heart and give up right before their breakthrough comes.

The people working to rebuild the wall in Nehemiah's time understood their need for renewed strength. They were constantly ridiculed for even thinking they could restore their city.

The teasing and taunts fell on deaf ears, however. God's people asked their loving Father for strength, and the wall was rebuilt. *"They all were trying to make us afraid, saying, 'Their hands will be weakened in the work, and it will not be done,'"* Nehemiah wrote, describing this. His response was a prayer: *"Now therefore, O God, strengthen my hands"* (Nehemiah 6:9).

Thankfully, Nehemiah and his comrades discovered that the joy of the Lord was their strength (Nehemiah 8:10). They overcame the taunts of their enemies and completed the wall.

If you need increased strength and endurance as you intercede for your city and nation today, meditate on God's wonderful promise in Isaiah 40:28-31:

Have you not known? Have you not heard? The everlasting God, the LORD, the Creator of the ends of the earth, neither faints nor is weary. His understanding is unsearchable. He gives power to the weak, And to those who have no might He increases strength.

Even the youths shall faint and be weary, and the young men shall utterly fall, but those who wait on the LORD shall renew their strength; they shall mount up with wings like eagles, they shall run and not be weary, they shall walk and not faint.

What a relief to know that additional strength is available when you are feeling weary or discouraged. When you take time to rest in His presence, God will fill you with His supernatural strength.

PRAYING THE LORD'S PRAYER

When discouragement threatens to derail your prayers, remember that Jesus gave us a model prayer to follow in Matthew 6:9-13, often called the Lord's Prayer. If you are new to prayer and intercession, this is a great way to pray for your personal life and your loved ones. But here are some ways you can apply this prayer to your intercession for your neighborhood, city, and nation:

Our Father...

> Lord, thank You for being my loving Heavenly Father. I pray for all my brothers and sisters in Christ today, asking that they be drawn near to You. I also pray that your

father-heart will draw prodigals home, welcoming them into Your Kingdom.

...in heaven...

Thank You, Father, that You reign and rule over all creation as the King of kings and Lord of lords. Thank You that Your sovereignty extends over every problem in my life and in my city and nation.

...hallowed be Your name.

Thank You for adopting me into Your family and giving me the powerful name of Jesus to use in my prayers, my warfare against the enemy, and my daily life.

Your kingdom come. Your will be done on earth as it is in heaven.

I pray that my city and nation will increasingly reflect Your will and the values of Your Kingdom. Just as there is no crime, sickness, poverty, or strife in Heaven, I pray that the society around me will reflect Your Heavenly realm more and more.

Give us this day our daily bread.

Thank You for providing for all my material needs today. I pray for my fellow Believers and fellow citizens to likewise experience Your bountiful provision.

And forgive us our debts, as we forgive our debtors.

Because of the blood of Jesus shed on the cross, I ask You to forgive my sins and the sins of my nation. I also choose to forgive my nation's leaders and anyone who has offended or wronged me.

And do not lead us into temptation, but deliver us from the evil one.

Father, I want to approach You today with *"clean hands and a pure heart"* (Psalm 24:3-5). As King David prayed, I ask You to create a clean heart in me and keep me from temptation (Psalm 51:10-12). Thank You for Your promise that I can discern Satan's schemes (2 Corinthians 2:11) and overcome him through the blood of

Jesus and the word of my testimony (Revelation 12:11). I ask You to have mercy on my city and nation, giving our leaders wisdom and keeping them from temptation. May the blood of Your Son be applied to any areas of sin or unrighteous. And may the schemes of the evil one be exposed as You shine Your light into every situation.

For Yours is the kingdom and the power and the glory forever. Amen.

Father, I worship and glorify You in my prayers, and I want to see You glorified through every other area of my life as well (1 Corinthians 10:31). Make me a faithful representative and ambassador for Your Kingdom in my community, my city, and my nation (2 Corinthians 5:20).

SOME ADDITIONAL SCRIPTURES ON PRAYER

"Seek the LORD and His strength; seek His face evermore!" – 1 Chronicles 16:11

"Hear, O LORD, when I cry with my voice! Have mercy also upon me, and answer me. When You said, 'Seek My face,' my heart said to You, 'Your face, Lord, I will seek.'" – Psalm 27:7-8

"Hear me when I call, O God of my righteousness! You have relieved me in my distress; Have mercy on me, and hear my prayer." – Psalm 4:1

"The LORD is far from the wicked, but he hears the prayer of the righteous." – Proverbs 15:29

"The LORD is near to all who call on Him, to all who call on Him in truth." – Psalm 145:18

"Continue earnestly in prayer, being vigilant in it with thanksgiving." – Colossians 4:2

Prayers for Specific Purposes

"Be anxious for nothing, but in everything by prayer and supplication, with thanksgiving, let your requests be made known to God; and the peace of God, which surpasses all understanding, will guard your hearts and minds through Christ Jesus. Finally, brethren, whatever things are true, whatever things are noble, whatever things are just, whatever things are pure, whatever things are lovely, whatever things are of good report, if there is any virtue and if there is anything praiseworthy—meditate on these things."
–Philippians 4:6-8

"Pray without ceasing." – 1 Thessalonians 5:17

"I desire therefore that the men pray everywhere, lifting up holy hands, without wrath and doubting."
– 1 Timothy 2:8

"Confess your trespasses to one another, and pray for one another, that you may be healed. The effective, fervent prayer of a righteous man avails much." – James 5:16

"Now it came to pass in those days that He went out to the mountain to pray, and continued all night in prayer to God."
– Luke 6:12

"Now in the morning, having risen a long while before daylight, He went out and departed to a solitary place; and there He prayed." – Mark 1:35

"Then He spoke a parable to them, that men always ought to pray and not lose heart." – Luke 18:1

"Wait on the LORD; be of good courage, and He shall strengthen your heart; wait, I say, on the LORD!" – Psalm 27:14

"Then you will call upon Me and go and pray to Me, and I will listen to you. And you will seek Me and find Me, when you search for Me with all your heart. I will be found by you, says the LORD, and I will bring you back from your captivity."
– Jeremiah 29:12-14

"Call to Me, and I will answer you, and show you great and mighty things, which you do not know." – Jeremiah 33:3

A Word from Our Founder

Dear friends,

I pray that God has stirred your heart by this message of hope and encouragement on how to spark a spiritual awakening in your nation. The Bible is clear: As God's children we must humble ourselves and pray. We must seek His face and turn from our wicked ways.

When we follow this powerful formula, the Lord has promised to hear our prayers and heal our land. The needs are great in every nation, so there's no time to waste.

At Inspiration Ministries, we recognize the power unleashed when Believers join together and pray prayers of agreement (Matthew 18:18-19). On page 146 you will find information on how to contact the prayer ministers in our International Prayer Center to join you in interceding for your nation.

God bless you!

David Cerullo

Inspiration Ministries
Founder and CEO

David Cerullo is the Founder, Chairman, and CEO of Inspiration Ministries located in Indian Land, South Carolina — a ministry dedicated to impacting people for Christ worldwide through media since 1990. David took a less traditional approach to ministry, graduating from Oral Roberts University with a degree in business administration and management. He has authored more than 20 different books and has been honored with an honorary Doctor of Ministry degree. He has been married to his wife Barbara for more than 40 years, and together they have two adult children and five grandchildren.

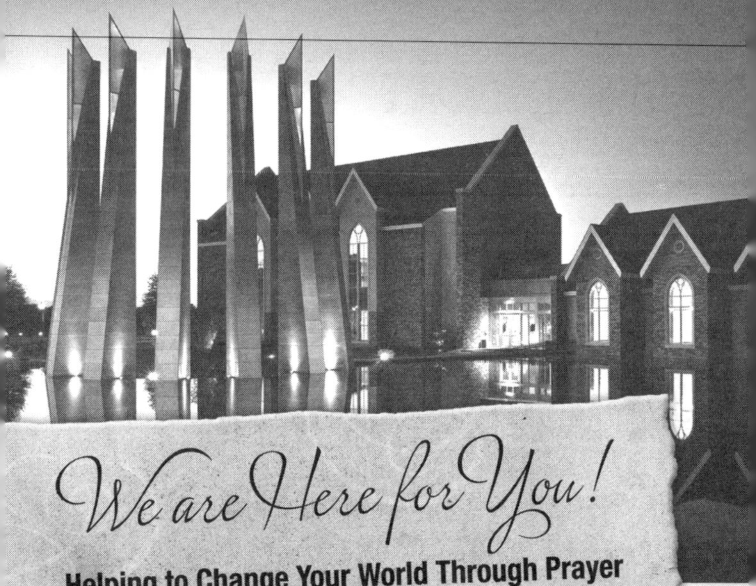

We are Here for You!
Helping to Change Your World Through Prayer

Do you need someone to pray with you about a financial need…a physical healing…an addiction…a broken relationship…or your spiritual growth with the Lord?

Our prayer ministers at the International Prayer Center are here for you. Because of God's goodness and faithfulness, His ears are attentive to the prayers made in this place (2 Chronicles 6:40).

"God does tremendous things as we pray for our Inspiration Partners over the phone. It's such a joy to see people reaching out to touch the Lord through prayer, and in return, to see God embrace them and meet their needs."
– TERESA, Prayer Minister

To contact our International Prayer Center, visit **inspiration.org/prayer** or call TODAY…

United States:
+1 803-578-1800

United Kingdom:
0845 683 0584

Canada:
(877) 261-3937

International:
+800 9982 4677

Caribbean:
877-487-7782

Every day, Souls are being saved, miracles are taking place, and people are being impacted for God's eternal Kingdom! We continually receive amazing testimonies like these from people whose lives have been touched by our faithful prayer ministers:

Debt cancelled… *"After you prayed with me, I received the cancellation of a $23,000 medical bill. The hospital called it an act of charity, but I say it was God!"* – MELVIN, New York

Son found… *"I had not heard from my son for five years, but I miraculously found him just two weeks after your prayer minister called!"* – Z.C., Missouri

Cancer gone… *"Thank you for standing with me in prayer and agreeing with me for my healing. The Lord has healed me of breast cancer!"* – NORMA, Michigan

Family restored… *"Thanks so much for your prayers. I've got my family back! The Lord gave me a great job, my wife was willing to take me back, and I've been clean from drugs and alcohol for almost a year. God is so good to us!"* – L.B., Colorado

This could be YOUR day for a miracle!
Let our prayer ministers intercede with God on your behalf, praying the Prayer of Agreement for the breakthrough you need.

READY FOR YOUR BREAKTHROUGH?

BREAK THROUGH: 20 Surprising Ways to Unleash Heaven's Resources reveals life-changing Biblical principles…

- How you can impact your family, finances, health, career, and spiritual life through "breakthrough prayers."

- The specific steps you can take to release more of God's favor in your life.

- How your life will change when you discover your new identity in Christ.

"With God ALL THINGS are possible!"
– Mark 10:27

Call one of these numbers to Sow a Seed for Souls and receive one or more of these life-changing ministry resources as a THANK YOU GIFT for partnering with us to impact people for Christ Worldwide!

God Has Made Appointments To Bless YOU!

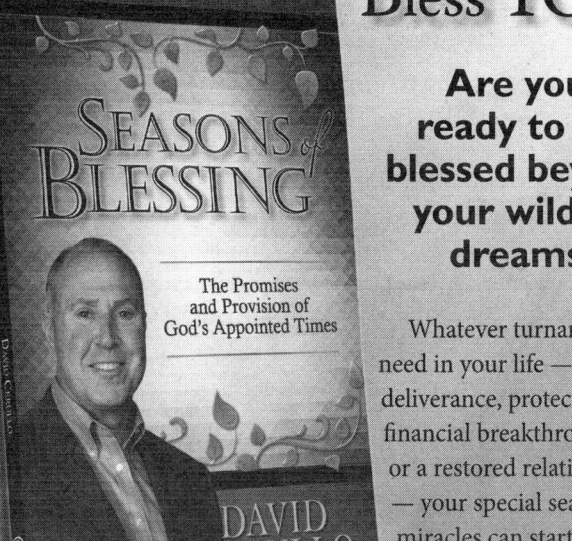

Are you ready to be blessed beyond your wildest dreams?

Whatever turnaround you need in your life — healing, deliverance, protection, a financial breakthrough, or a restored relationship — your special season of miracles can start with a step of faith TODAY!

David Cerullo's powerful book is filled with Biblical secrets that will transform your life through the special times each year when God wants to meet with you and bless you in extraordinary ways.

"These are the appointed feasts of the LORD that you shall proclaim as holy convocations; they are My appointed feasts."

– Leviticus 23:2-3

United States: +1 803-578-1899

United Kingdom: 0845 683 0580

Canada: (877) 255-3205

International: +800 9982 4677

Caribbean: 877-487-7782

DISCOVER YOUR LIFE'S MISSING INGREDIENT!

In *The Favor Factor*, David Cerullo explains how the favor of God will reverse every negative circumstance and propel you to the life of your dreams.

He offers powerful Biblical keys for unleashing the favor of God and experiencing His blessings, peace, and provision in every area of your life.

God's favor is the missing ingredient that can change *everything* — transforming your health, finances, emotions, and relationships forever!

Call one of these numbers to Sow a Seed for Souls
and receive one or more of these life-changing ministry resources as a
THANK YOU GIFT for partnering with us to impact people for Christ Worldwide!

United States:	*United Kingdom:*	*Canada:*
+1 803-578-1899	0845 683 0580	(877) 255-3205

International:	*Caribbean:*
+800 9982 4677	877-487-7782